Chairman Chaffetz, Ranking Member Cummings, and Members of the Committee,

I am pleased to be here today to discuss SIGAR's inspections of facilities and infrastructure built and renovated by the Department of Defense (DOD) using reconstruction funds.

After the Taliban was driven from power in 2001, the United States, along with other coalition partners, initiated projects to help reconstruct Afghanistan, which had been devastated by nearly 30 years of conflict. Through December 31, 2015, Congress had appropriated about $113.1 billion for reconstruction activities in Afghanistan. The Department of Defense (DOD), the Department of State, and the U.S. Agency for International Development have carried out most of those reconstruction activities, which include capacity building programs; economic development projects; the acquisition of vehicles, equipment and clothing for the Afghan National Defense and Security Forces (ANDSF); and construction and renovation projects for various types of facilities and infrastructure for both ANSDF and civilian use.

Since its creation in 2008, SIGAR has issued 37 inspection reports examining 45 DOD reconstruction projects with a combined value of about $1.1 billion.[1] The projects were located in 15 of Afghanistan's 34 provinces, and included 16 Afghan National Police (ANP) and 13 Afghan National Army (ANA) bases, 5 schools, 3 medical facilities, 3 incinerator locations, 2 storage facilities, 1 road, 1 bridge, and 1 electrical plant. These projects do not constitute a representative sample of all DOD reconstruction projects. As a result, we do not use our findings to draw conclusions about the full population of DOD reconstruction projects. However, our findings provide valuable insight into the varying quality of projects that exist and the reasons for these project outcomes. Figure 1 shows the location of each of the 45 DOD reconstruction projects we inspected.

My testimony today will discuss our March 11, 2016, report that analyzes and identifies common themes across the 36 inspection reports we issued from July 2009 through September 2015.[2] It also includes findings from our more recent inspection of the Afghan Ministry of Defense (MOD) headquarters building located in Kabul.[3]

---

[1] From July 2009 through September 2015, we completed 12 inspections of Department of State and U.S. Agency for International Development reconstruction projects. We plan to issue an analysis of those reports in mid-2016.

[2] SIGAR 16-22-IP, *Department of Defense Reconstruction Projects: Summary of SIGAR Inspection Reports Issued from July 2009 through September 2015*, March 11, 2016.

[3] SIGAR 16-16-IP, *Afghan Ministry of Defense Headquarters: $154.7 Million Building Appears Well Built, but Has Several Construction Issues that Should Be Assessed*, February 11, 2016.

Figure 1 - DOD Projects SIGAR Has Inspected Since 2009

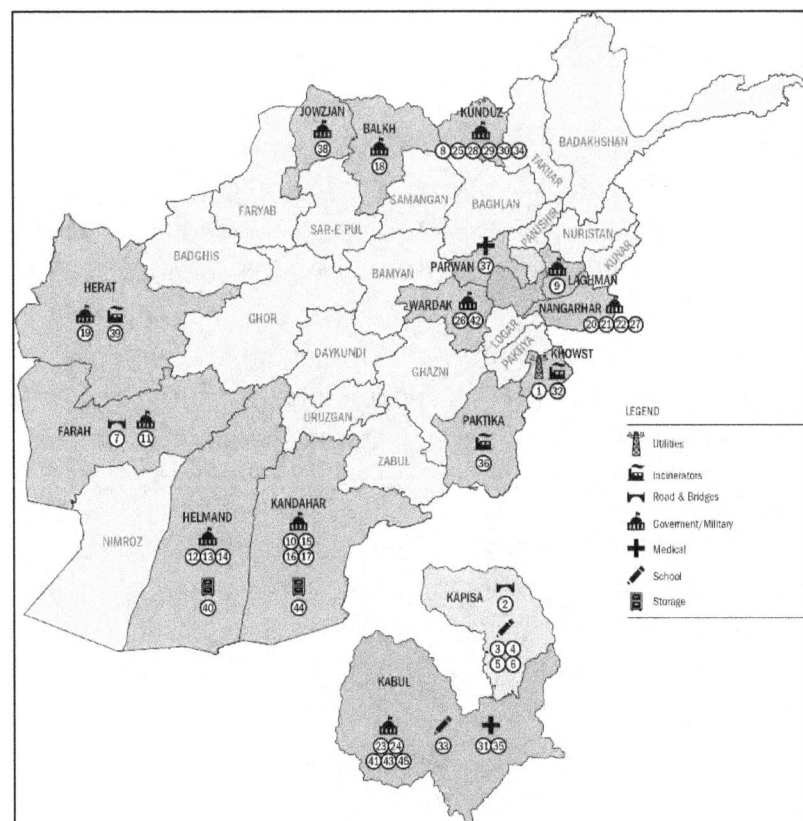

Source: SIGAR analysis

Notes: This map is not intended to show the exact location of the projects. It solely indicates the provinces in which the projects are located. The numbers on the map correspond to the projects we inspected and the order in which those inspections occurred. Appendix I lists each project and its corresponding map number.

Background

Two of DOD's reconstruction objectives in Afghanistan were to (1) train, equip, base, and sustain the Afghan National Defense and Security Forces (ANDSF), comprised of the ANA and ANP, and (2) respond to urgent humanitarian relief and small-scale reconstruction projects to support local Afghan communities.[4] The majority of all U.S. reconstruction funding—about $72.4 billion, or more than 64 percent, of the $113.1 billion appropriated as

---

[4] The ANA and ANP were known collectively as the Afghan National Security Forces until 2015, when the name was changed to the Afghan National Defense and Security Forces.

of December 2015—has been allocated to DOD to accomplish these missions. DOD's reconstruction projects primarily have been funded through the Afghanistan Security Forces Fund (ASFF) ($63.9 billion) and the Commander's Emergency Response Program (CERP) ($3.7 billion).[5]

Congress created the ASFF to provide the ANDSF with equipment, supplies, services, training, and salaries, as well as facility and infrastructure repair, renovation, and construction. Through December 31, 2015, DOD had disbursed about $56.2 billion of ASFF funds. The largest portion of funds disbursed from the ASFF, or about $37.6 billion, went to sustain the ANA; $18.2 billion went to sustain the ANP; and the remaining $387.4 million went to related activities. DOD also reported that through this same time period, it disbursed approximately $5.7 billion from the ASFF to support infrastructure projects for the ANDSF. These projects included, among other things, military headquarters, barracks, schools and other training facilities, police checkpoint structures, airfields, and roads.

CERP was established in 2003, under the Coalition Provisional Authority in Iraq, to enable military commanders to respond to urgent humanitarian relief requirements in Iraq and Afghanistan.[6] Congress has appropriated approximately $3.7 billion for CERP in Afghanistan, and, as of December 31, 2015, DOD reported that about $2.3 billion of those funds had been expended. CERP funds generally are intended for use on small-scale projects, which are estimated to cost less than $500,000, though CERP funds have been spent on many projects that cost more than that amount. Program guidance restricts CERP to 20 authorized purposes, including electricity, transportation, education, healthcare, and water and sanitation projects. U.S. commanders have used CERP to fund projects in all 34 provinces in Afghanistan.

The U.S. Central Command is responsible for military activities in southwest Asia, and, therefore, has Afghanistan within its area of responsibility. Within Afghanistan, U.S. Forces–Afghanistan (USFOR-A) has overall responsibility for military operations, including DOD's reconstruction program. The Combined Security Transition Command–Afghanistan (CSTC-A), under USFOR-A's command, has responsibility for funding the country-wide building program to support the national, regional, and district-level operations of the ANDSF. With regards to implementation, the U.S. Army Corps of Engineers (USACE) has been responsible for awarding contracts for and overseeing most of the reconstruction projects funded through the ASFF. The Air Force Civil Engineer Center (AFCEC), previously the Air Force Center for

---

[5] DOD also received funding to support its reconstruction efforts in Afghanistan from several other sources, such as the Afghanistan Infrastructure Fund. Combined, the other sources of funding totaled $4.7 billion through December 31, 2015.

[6] The Coalition Provisional Authority was established as the transitional government of Iraq following the U.S. invasion of Iraq in March 2003.

Engineering and the Environment (AFCEE), has also awarded several reconstruction contracts.[7] USFOR-A components, such as joint task forces and provincial reconstruction teams, have been involved in administering most of the contracts for and overseeing CERP-funded projects.[8]

SIGAR's Inspection Program

SIGAR began its inspections of DOD reconstruction projects in May 2009 and issued its first inspection report in July 2009.[9] Our inspections are assessments of facilities and infrastructure built or renovated using reconstruction funds. Generally, our inspection objectives are to determine the extent to which (1) construction met contract requirements and technical specifications, and (2) facilities were being used by their intended recipients. As part of this assessment, we determine, among other things, whether the facilities are structurally sound and completed on time and within budget.

Prior to visiting a project site, our inspection team reviews project documents, including, when available, the construction contract, modifications to the contract, design drawings, applicable international and DOD building codes, and quality assurance and other oversight reports. Reviewing these documents helps to identify specific criteria for determining whether construction was performed according to contract requirements, and, if not, whether the responsible administering agency provided adequate project oversight. During the on-site visits, our inspection team examines the quality of the construction to determine such things as whether the facilities are (1) in compliance with contract requirements and technical specifications, (2) structurally sound, (3) complete, and (4) being used. In addition to inspecting the facilities, when appropriate, the team obtains views about the project from contractors as well as U.S. and Afghan government officials.

Depending on the outcomes of our inspections, we may make recommendations to improve the efficiency and effectiveness of construction efforts. We have an established

---

[7] On October 1, 2012, the Air Force Center for Engineering and the Environment, the Air Force Civil Engineer Support Agency, and the Air Force Real Property Agency merged to become the Air Force Civil Engineer Center.

[8] Provincial reconstruction teams were key instruments through which the international community delivered assistance at the provincial and district level. The U.S.-managed provincial reconstruction teams were interim organizations used to improve security, support good governance, and enhance provincial development.

[9] SIGAR Inspection 09-01, *Inspection of Improvements to the Khowst City Electrical Power System: Safety and Sustainability Issues Were Not Adequately Addressed*, July 28, 2009.

recommendation follow-up process with DOD to track the corrective actions taken or target dates for completing the corrective actions for each recommendation.[10]

Our inspections were conducted under the authority of Public Law No. 110-181, as amended, and the Inspector General Act of 1978, as amended. Of the 37 inspections SIGAR conducted since 2009, 28 were completed in accordance with Quality Standards for Inspection and Evaluation, published by the Council of the Inspectors General on Integrity and Efficiency (CIGIE). The 9 remaining inspections were conducted in accordance with generally accepted government auditing standards (GAGAS). The engineering assessments were conducted by our professional engineers in accordance with the National Society of Professional Engineers' Code of Ethics for Engineers. Appendix I lists the 37 inspection reports we have completed on DOD reconstruction projects, including their respective costs, administering agency, findings, and recommendations. Appendix II lists the reports and information about whether the facilities were built as required and were being used at the time of our inspections.

Impact of the Military Drawdown in Afghanistan

With the drawdown of U.S. and coalition forces beginning in June 2011, significant portions of Afghanistan became inaccessible to SIGAR and others conducting oversight of reconstruction activities, as well as the agencies implementing reconstruction efforts. For the majority of DOD reconstruction project inspections, we were able to personally visit the project site. However, security concerns on the ground sometimes limited our inspection teams' ability to conduct on-site project assessments. For example, in some cases, we had a limited amount of time on site to perform our inspections because of security and other concerns.

Further, as time went on, with the drawdown of U.S. forces combined with the increase in insurgent activity, we were not able to reach some project locations to conduct a physical inspection. For example, our inspections team was scheduled to visit the Gereshk Cold and Dry Storage Facility project site in Helmand province on two occasions in January and March 2014. Although the site was located within an area that allowed civilian visits when security conditions were deemed to be safe, both visit requests were denied. International Security Assistance Force officials told us that the requests were denied because that area had high insurgent activity and was unsafe to visit. Instead, we relied heavily on an extensive

---

[10] For a detailed explanation of SIGAR's recommendation follow-up process, see SIGAR 15-29-AR, *Department of Defense: More than 75 Percent of All SIGAR Audit and Inspection Report Recommendations Have Been Implemented*, January 15, 2015.

collection of contract and management documentation, including photos and site visit reports, as well as information from Afghan government officials.

Our ability to access project sites in Kabul has even been limited. For example, during our inspection of the MOD headquarters building, despite having military logistics support, we had to reschedule some of our site visits multiple times due to security conditions.

As an alternative means for conducting oversight, due to a limited ability to travel within Afghanistan, we have hired Afghan engineers and analysts to assist with our inspection work, with four currently on staff. In addition, in December 2014, we entered into an agreement with vetted and well-trained Afghan civil society partners to assist us with our inspections. These partners conduct site visits and engineering assessments of various reconstruction projects on our behalf and report back to us on the results. We have assigned an agreement officer to work closely with those partners to ensure their work meets GAGAS or CIGIE Quality Standards for Inspection and Evaluation, in addition to SIGAR's internal quality control requirements. Through this partnership, in 2015, we were able to expand our oversight coverage, and we plan to increase our coverage even further in 2016.

Most of the Facilities SIGAR Inspected Did Not Meet Contract Requirement or Technical Specifications

Of the 45 DOD reconstruction projects we inspected, 17 met contract requirements and technical specifications. These projects demonstrate that high-quality work can be completed when contractors adhere to requirements and there is adequate oversight. Afghan support can also have a positive impact on the outcome of a project. For example, in April 2013, we reported that the Qala-i-Muslim medical clinic in Kabul province appeared to be a success story.[11] The community of 4,000 people supported the clinic's construction, and a villager donated the land. During our inspection, we did not observe any major deficiencies and found that the clinic had working heat, electrical, and water systems; floors were clean; bedding was plentiful and well kept; and the separate pharmacy building was well stocked. We also noted that the Afghan Ministry of Public Health had signed an agreement as part of the approval process to sustain the clinic upon completion and that it had fulfilled its commitment to do so.

---

[11] SIGAR Inspection 13-07, *Qala-i-Muslim Medical Clinic: Serving the Community Well, But Construction Quality Could Not Be Fully Assessed*, April 17, 2013.

In our October 2009 inspection of the $6.6 million Mahmood Raqi to Nijrab road project in Kapisa province, we reported that the project, which was administered by the Kapisa provincial reconstruction team, was on schedule, and the Afghan contractor was adhering to Afghan road construction standards to grade and widen the road to meet alignment and road width requirements.[12] We spot checked the base course construction in three places and found that the thickness and width conformed to the standards. In another example, the contractor was responsible for repairing, constructing, or extending 58 culverts along the roadway, as well as repairing and resurfacing five existing bridges and constructing a new 16-meter long bridge.[13] We determined that the level of workmanship was adequate and found no major deficiencies in the design or construction of the culverts or bridge work.

During our recent inspection of the $154.7 million MOD headquarters building, we determined that the building generally met contract requirements and technical specifications. However, we identified some deficiencies that could affect the building's structural integrity during an earthquake or prolonged periods of rain.[14] Specifically, we found issues with building separation joints needed for seismic activity; equipment without lateral bracing, which is needed for seismic activity; inadequate roof drains to remove storm water; and stairway handrails that were installed below the required height.

The 28 remaining projects had construction work that did not meet contract requirements or technical specifications. The deficiencies we found during these inspections generally fit into three categories:

1. Soil issues, including inadequate site preparation and collapsible soil due to poor grading.

2. Systems problems related, but not limited to, electrical, water, and sewer distribution, including improperly installed heating, cooling, and ventilation systems; inoperable water systems; improper testing and commissioning of mechanical systems; and non-code-compliant electrical wiring.

3. Structural problems, such as the use of sub-standard, inadequate, and irregular building materials; poorly mixed, cured, and reinforced concrete; and improperly installed roofs, which led to leaks.

---

[12] SIGAR Inspection 09-02, *Inspection of Mahmood Raqi to Nijrab Road Project in Kapisa Province: Contract Requirements Met; but Sustainability Concerns Exist*, October 2, 2009

[13] A culvert is a structure that allows water to flow under a road from one side to the other side, and can be made from a pipe, reinforced concrete, or other material.

[14] SIGAR 16-16-IP, *Afghan Ministry of Defense Headquarters: $154.7 Million Building Appears Well Built, but Has Several Construction Issues that Should Be Assessed*, February 11, 2016.

We found that poor contractor performance and inadequate government oversight were the primary contributors to non-adherence to contract requirements and technical specifications.

Of the 28 projects, 16 had deficiencies so severe that they threatened the structural integrity of the buildings and the safety of their occupants. For example, during our January 2013 inspection of the Bathkhak School in Kabul province, we found that the contractor substituted a concrete slab roof for the wood-trussed roof required by the contract, raising safety concerns for the occupants due to the school's location in an area of high seismic activity.[15] We also found construction flaws that could compromise the school's structural integrity, including large gaps between bricks in the walls that supported the concrete roof; walls that did not appear to be reinforced; and honeycombing, exposed rebar, and concrete form boards remaining in the concrete slab roof. These deficiencies were so serious and potentially life threatening that we sent a safety alert letter to the Commander of USFOR-A, urging a delay in the transfer of the newly constructed school buildings to the Afghan government until our inspection report was issued and the Commander could take action to address the full set of concerns discussed in the report.[16]

In our January 2015 inspection report on the nearly $500,000 Afghan Special Police Training Center's dry fire range, we reported that the buildings in the facility began to disintegrate within 4 months of the range's completion.[17] This disintegration, or "melting," occurred because Qesmatullah Nasrat Construction Company, an Afghan firm, failed to adhere to contract requirements and international building standards, and used substandard materials. We also found poor government oversight throughout all phases of the project. Specifically, the contracting officer's representatives failed to identify any construction deficiencies. Further, despite the deficiencies, the Regional Contracting Center accepted the facilities and failed to hold the contractor fully accountable for correcting those deficiencies before the contract warranty expired. As a result, the range's safety and long-term sustainability were compromised. The Afghan government had to demolish and rebuild the dry fire range using its own funds, resulting in a waste of U.S. taxpayers' money.

DOD has taken some steps to improve its processes to enhance control and accountability for its projects. For example, as soon as we informed USACE of the lack of water at the Afghan Border Police Base Lal Por 2, it assembled a project development team to find a

---

[15] SIGAR Inspection 13-10, *Bathkhak School: Unauthorized Contract Design Changes and Poor Construction Could Compromise Structural Integrity*, July 24, 2013.

[16] SIGAR SP-13-5, *Safety Alert Letter: Bathkhak School*, June 21, 2013.

[17] SIGAR 15-27-IP, *Afghan Special Police Training Center's Dry Fire Range: Poor Contractor Performance and Poor Government Oversight Led to Project Failure*, January 13, 2015.

solution to the lack of water issue that prevented Lal Por 2 from being used.[18] In June 2011, USACE noted that it began mandating hydro-geologist reviews to assess the water supply as part of its site assessments. In 2012, after several of our reports identified missing contract and project documentation as a problem that affected our ability to perform complete and thorough audits and inspections, USACE issued a new policy for the certification and training of contracting officer's representatives, particularly to emphasize the importance of documentation in their files.

Further, USFOR-A stated in comments to our Abdul Manan School inspection report in 2009 that provincial reconstruction teams without engineer and construction inspectors drawn from military organizations should not be allowed to conduct construction-related CERP initiatives.[19] During that inspection, we found that the facility was not built as required and was not being used. Further, the contract's Statement of Work did not include major construction elements, resulting in a contract modification and cost increase. It was later determined that the contract was in violation of CERP guidelines, resulting in the termination of the contract and the project being re-bid.[20]

Despite DOD's efforts to establish procedures and improve processes, serious problems continued with its reconstruction projects. For example, CSTC-A acknowledged that in 2009, it "only had about thirty personnel to manage the program, a clearly insufficient number to both plan and execute." However, CSTC-A added that it had taken, and continued to take, multiple actions to improve required oversight, including obtaining more personnel to do it.[21] CSTC-A stated that it had begun to expand its engineering staff from 30 in early 2010 to 96 in early 2011, and was trying to secure an additional 66 engineers. In addition, the command noted changes in management and contracting guidance designed to improve planning and oversight.

However, problems persisted. For example, construction of the Afghan Special Police's Dry Fire Range and the Bathkhak School started in 2012. We identified unapproved product substitution as a problem with both projects, an issue we had raised in prior reports. In our July 2013 quarterly report to Congress, we wrote that "Investigations, along with SIGAR's

---

[18] SIGAR Inspection 12-01, *Construction Deficiencies at Afghan Border Police Bases Put $19 Million Investment at Risk*, July 30, 2012.

[19] SIGAR Inspection 10-02, *Inspection of Abdul Manan Secondary School Construction Project in Kapisa Province: Insufficient Planning, Safety Problems, and Poor Quality Control Affect Project Results*, October 26, 2009.

[20] The initial contract was awarded to the Provincial Director of Education as the prime contractor in September 2008. Revised CERP guidelines issued by U.S. Central Command in late 2008 prohibited line ministries from serving as contracting parties for projects funded by CERP. As a result, the original contract was terminated, and a new contract was put out for bid.

[21] SIGAR Audit 11-6, *Inadequate Planning for ANSF Facilities Increases Risk for $11.4 Billion Program*, January 26, 2011.

audits, inspections, and special projects, highlight serious shortcomings in U.S. oversight of contracts: poor planning, delayed or inadequate inspections, insufficient documentation, dubious decisions, and—perhaps most troubling—a pervasive lack of accountability."[22,23]

At the Time of SIGAR's Inspections, About One-third of the 22 Completed Projects Were Not Being Used, and 23 Projects Were Incomplete

Of the 45 DOD reconstruction projects that we inspected, at the time of our inspections, 22 were complete and 23 were incomplete. Of the 22 projects that were complete, 15 were being used and 7, or about one-third of the completed projects, had never been used. We found that usage of the 15 projects varied with some projects being fully used and others only partially used. For example, the Qala-i-Muslim Medical Clinic was being fully used when we inspected it. During our January 2013 site inspection, the clinic director told us that the clinic was serving between 200 and 300 patients per month.[24] Records we reviewed indicated that 1,565 outpatient consultations, 63 prenatal patients, and 63 newborn deliveries had occurred since the clinic opened in September 2011.

In other cases, we found the facilities were completed but were only partially being used, such as the MOD headquarters building, the Salang hospital, and the Iman Sahib Border Police Headquarters. For example, in January 2014, we reported that although the Salang hospital in Parwan province was being used, it was not providing many of the services that it was intended to provide.[25] In addition, the hospital staff were only using about 35 percent of the square footage of the constructed facility, and the hospital employed less than 20 percent of the staff it was expected to employ. According to the doctors and nurses on site during our inspection, the limited use—due primarily to the lack of electricity, water, furniture, and equipment—had prevented them from providing optimal medical care. For example, because there was no clean water, hospital staff were washing newborns with untreated river water.

Seven of the 14 completed projects had never been used at the time of our inspection. For example, in October 2013, we reported that the Walayatti Medical Clinic had not been used

---

[22] See SIGAR, *Quarterly Report to the United States Congress*, July 30, 2013.

[23] The DOD Inspector General found similar recurring problems in construction for the U.S. military (see DODIG-2015-059, *Military Construction in a Contingency Environment: Summary of Weaknesses Identified in Reports Issued From January 1, 2008, Through March 31, 2014*, January 9, 2015).

[24] SIGAR Inspection 13-07, *Qala-i-Muslim Medical Clinic: Serving the Community Well, But Construction Quality Could Not Be Fully Assessed*, April 17, 2013.

[25] SIGAR 14-31-IP, *Salang Hospital: Lack of Water and Power Severely Limits Hospital Services, and Major Construction Deficiencies Raise Safety Concerns*, January 29, 2014.

despite having been completed 20 months earlier.[26] The clinic had no medical equipment and had not been staffed. Further, there was no evidence that the clinic had been properly transferred to the Afghan government or that the Ministry of Public Health planned to supply equipment for or staff the clinic. A ministry official told us that the clinic was not included in the ministry's operation and maintenance plan because the U.S. government had failed to coordinate with the Ministry of Public Health's Policy and Planning Directorate, and had not officially transferred the facility to the Afghan government. The project files contained no documentation of the clinic's transfer to the Afghan government after construction was completed.

In July 2014, we reported that the Gereshk Cold and Dry Storage Facility in Helmand province—a $2.89 million facility funded by DOD's Task Force for Business and Stability Operations (TFBSO) and built under a USACE-administered contract—had been completed and was well constructed, but had never been used and was not being maintained.[27] Construction was completed in May 2013, and the storage facility was transferred to the Afghan government in September 2013. However, TFBSO did not achieve what it told us was the key to the project's success—the operation, maintenance, and control of the facility by an Afghan business. The Afghan Ministry of Commerce and Industry was still looking for private-sector investors.

Of the 23 projects that were incomplete at the time of our inspection, 6 projects were still under construction within their originally scheduled completion dates and, therefore, would not have been ready for use at the time we inspected them. These were the Habib Rahman Secondary School, the Kohi Girls' School, the Tojg Bridge, the ANA Garrison at Gamberi, the ANP Main Road Security Company, and the Bathkhak School. Five projects were incomplete due to project termination or for reasons we could not determine at the time of our inspections. For example, the ANA slaughterhouse project was terminated before completion. The 12 remaining projects were experiencing construction delays that had extended their completion past their original schedules. Seven of the 23 projects were being used to some extent at the time of our inspections. For example, despite being incomplete, ANA personnel were using the ANA Garrison at Kunduz.

With respect to the 12 projects experiencing construction delays, we determined that at the time of our inspections, the delays ranged from 5 months to over 2 years and 7 months beyond the projects' originally scheduled completion dates. The primary factors contributing

---

[26] SIGAR 14-10-IP, *Walayatti Medical Clinic: Facility Was Not Constructed According to Design Specifications and Has Never Been Used*, October 30, 2013

[27] SIGAR 14-82-IP, *Gereshk Cold and Dry Storage Facility: Quality of Construction Appears To Be Good, but the Facility Has Not Been Used to Date*, July 16, 2014.

to delays included poor contractor performance, insurgent activity, inclement weather, and contract modifications, as well as inadequate planning and oversight. For example, the ANP provincial headquarters in Kunduz was not complete and was experiencing construction delays of about 1 year at the time of our on-site inspection.[28]

During our review of construction at the Kabul Military Training Center, we found that about 80 percent of all AFCEE projects constructed on CSTC-A's behalf had experienced schedule delays.[29] Although AFCEE has since taken corrective action, between 2006 and 2010, our review of AFCEE data showed that 33 of 41 AFCEE construction projects for CSTC-A were delayed. The delays, caused by a variety of factors including contractor performance problems, ranged from 1 month to 2 years, and averaged 10 months.

DOD Has Implemented the Majority of Recommendations Made in SIGAR's Inspection Reports

In our 37 inspection reports of DOD projects, we made 100 recommendations to the department to correct the construction deficiencies we identified and improve the efficiency and effectiveness of its reconstruction activities. As of February 26, 2016, we had closed 93 of those recommendations. Of those 100 recommendations, DOD concurred with and implemented 79 recommendations. Although DOD did not implement 14 of the remaining recommendations, we closed these recommendations because (1) DOD did not concur with the recommendation or took no action on the recommendation, and we believed no further action would be taken; (2) DOD did not take timely action, which rendered the recommendation moot; or (3) planned work superseded the recommendation.

As of February 26, 2016, seven recommendations remained open. This included five recommendations that were still within the initial 60-day period between report issuance and our initial follow up with DOD. Of the seven total open recommendations, we made five of those recommendations to U.S. Central Command subordinate commands and two to USACE. As part of our follow-up process, we will continue to monitor the open recommendations to determine if DOD is taking appropriate steps to implement the recommendations. Appendix I lists the recommendations we made by inspection report and the current status of those recommendations.

---

[28] SIGAR Inspection 13-4, *Kunduz Afghan National Police Provincial Headquarters: After Construction Delays and Cost Increases, Concerns Remain About the Facility's Usability and Sustainability*, January 24, 2013

[29] SIGAR Audit 12-02, *Better Planning and Oversight Could Have Reduced Construction Delays and Costs at the Kabul Military Training Center*, October 26, 2011.

The high implementation rate indicates that DOD was generally responsive to taking action to implement our recommendations. For example:

- CSTC-A agreed with our finding that the stairway handrails in the MOD headquarters building were installed below the required height and noted in its comments on a draft of our report that the contractor corrected the deficiency. We verified during a January 2016 follow up site visit that the handrails had been fixed.[30]
- USACE agreed with the deficiencies we identified at all three Afghan Border Police bases in Nangarhar province that we inspected, including critical water supply and septic and sewage system deficiencies. USACE noted that the contractor had corrected many of the deficiencies prior to the issuance of our report.[31] USACE also noted that it officially notified the contractor to remediate the remaining deficiencies within the contract warranty period and that it withheld almost $700,000 in retainage and liquidated damages pending satisfactory closeout submittal and approval.[32]
- USACE took immediate action at the ANA Garrison in Gamberi to (1) remedy possible flooding by having drainage areas examined and repaired, and have the contractor conduct frequent surveys for future deteriorating conditions; (2) repair a bridge near the garrison's main entrance that we believed could collapse under heavy traffic because its deck service had been compromised; and (3) designed and planned for the installation of a perimeter fence that we said was needed to secure the weapons training range.[33]
- The Kapisa provincial reconstruction team concurred with our recommendation to award a follow-up contract to repair the many deficiencies uncovered during our inspection at the Farukh Shah School, including the need to properly grade and compact the construction site's soil to prevent erosion from undermining the foundation of the school's various structures.[34]

Although DOD corrected some of the construction deficiencies, making the repairs sometimes resulted in additional expenditures beyond the initial cost of the contracts. For example, at the ANP provincial headquarters in Kunduz, USACE's failure to address potential collapsible soil conditions as part of its $12.4 million contract award caused a 10-month

---

[30] SIGAR 16-16-IP, *Afghan Ministry of Defense Headquarters: $154.7 Million Building Appears Well Built, but Has Several Construction Issues that Should Be Assessed*, February 11, 2016.

[31] Although we did not issue the final report until July 2012, in April 2012, we briefed USACE on the issues we identified during our site visits and potential solutions.

[32] SIGAR Inspection 12-01, *Construction Deficiencies at Afghan Border Police Bases Put $19 Million Investment at Risk*, July 30, 2012.

[33] SIGAR Audit 10-10, *ANA Garrison at Gamberi Appears Well Built Overall but Some Construction Issues Need to Be Addressed*, April 30, 2010.

[34] SIGAR Inspection 10-01, *Inspection of Farukh Shah School Construction Project in Kapisa Province: Project Completion Approved Before All Contract Requirements Met*, October 26, 2009.

delay in the project's completion and a $5 million cost increase.[35] In addition, repairs to the Farukh Shah School would require a follow-up contract beyond the $150,000 in CERP funds already spent. Our reports did not routinely break down additional repair costs since some projects were ongoing at the time of our inspections or additional contracts would occur after our inspections. As a result, we could not determine the total amount spent to make various repairs we identified.

SIGAR Remains Concerned about the Afghan Government's Ability to Maintain DOD-constructed Facilities

We have been expressing concern about the sustainability of facilities and infrastructure in Afghanistan since we issued our first inspection reports in 2009. For example, we noted that the Afghan government may have difficulty operating and maintaining the electrical power system in the city of Khowst, even after a $1.6 million contract to improve the system.[36] We also questioned the sustainability of the $6.6 million Mahmood Raqi to Nijrab road construction project in Kapisa province due to the demands that would be placed on the road and the inability of the local Afghan authorities to maintain improved roads due to a lack of proper equipment, material, personnel, and expertise.[37]

In our 2012 audit of two USACE-administered contracts for the operation and maintenance of ANDSF facilities across Afghanistan, we found that the Afghan government will likely be incapable of fully sustaining ANDSF facilities after the transition of security responsibility to the Afghans at the end of 2014 and the expected decrease in U.S. and coalition support.[38] The Afghan government's challenges in assuming O&M responsibilities include a lack of sufficient numbers and quality of personnel, as well as undeveloped budgeting, procurement, and logistics systems.

Recognizing the importance of the sustainability of facilities, infrastructure, and other reconstruction programs, in December 2014, we issued our first High-Risk List to call attention to program areas and elements of the U.S.-funded reconstruction effort in

---

[35] SIGAR Inspection 13-4, *Kunduz Afghan National Police Provincial Headquarters: After Construction Delays and Cost Increases, Concerns Remain about the Facility's Usability and Sustainability*, January 24, 2013.

[36] SIGAR Inspection 09-01, *Improvements to the Khowst City Electrical Power System: Safety and Sustainability Issues Were Not Adequately Addressed*, July 28, 2009.

[37] SIGAR Inspection 09-02, *Mahmood Raqi to Nijrab Road Construction Project in Kapisa Province: Contract Requirements Met, But Sustainability Concerns Exist*, October 2, 2009.

[38] SIGAR Audit 13-1, *Afghan National Security Forces Facilities: Concerns with Funding, Oversight, and Sustainability for Operation and Maintenance*, October 30, 2012.

Afghanistan that are especially vulnerable to significant waste, fraud, and abuse.[39] The list identifies seven key program areas that are essential to the success of the reconstruction effort. In other words, if there is a failure in any of these areas, the entire 13-year reconstruction effort could fail, resulting in billions of dollars in taxpayer funds being wasted. Sustainability is one of the key program areas we identified.[40] We noted that much of the more than $107 billion the United States had committed to reconstruction projects and programs as of December 2014 is at risk of being wasted because the Afghans cannot sustain the investment without significant support from the United States and other donors. Specifically, based on our work, we concluded that the Afghans lack the capacity—financial, technical, managerial, or otherwise—to operate and maintain much of what has been built or established during more than a decade of international assistance.

Because the Afghan government does not have the capacity to sustain ANDSF facilities, DOD has taken steps to ensure the operation and maintenance of these facilities until the Afghan government is able to do so itself. As noted above, since 2010, CSTC-A has funded contracts for the operation and maintenance of ANSDF facilities across Afghanistan. These contracts include a training component. Further, in 2012, DOD decided to reduce construction plans for ANDSF facilities for a variety of reasons, including the non-use and underutilization of existing facilities, as well as the drawdown of U.S. military and coalition forces anticipated by the end of 2014. For example, in April 2012, the International Security Assistance Force created the Operational Basing Board, which was expected to meet weekly to review and nominate existing U.S. and coalition facilities for closure or transfer to the Afghan government. As a result, through December 2012, the coalition closed 235 facilities and transferred 352 other facilities to the ANDSF. According to CSTC-A, transferring these existing coalition facilities to the ANDSF helped reduce plans to construct 318 new ANDSF facilities and decreased costs by approximately $2 billion.

Our September 2013 audit report addressing ANDSF facility planning identified 52 additional projects that might not meet the International Security Assistance Force's construction deadline, which was tied to the drawdown of U.S. and coalition forces anticipated by the end of 2014.[41] As a result, we recommended further planning and action

---

[39] SIGAR, *High-Risk List*, December 2014.

[40] The other six program areas are corruption/rule of law, ANDSF capacity and capabilities, on-budget support, counternarcotics, contract management and oversight access, and strategy and planning.

[41] SIGAR Audit 13-18, *Afghan National Security Forces: Additional Action Needed to Reduce Waste in $4.7 Billion Worth of Planned and Ongoing Construction Projects*, September 13, 2013. U.S. and coalition forces transferred security responsibility to the Afghan government at the end 2014. Leading up to this transition, those forces began to reduce their presence in Afghanistan. Because of this reduced U.S. and coalition presence, the International Security Assistance Force issued guidance requiring that all remaining ANDSF construction projects be completed by December 2014.

to reduce waste in $4.7 billion worth of planned and ongoing construction. Our conclusion noted:

> DOD is building these facilities without knowledge of current utilization and the Afghan government's ability to sustain them. We have previously reported that current facilities are underutilized or not being used at all, and have repeatedly questioned the ANDSF's ability to operate and maintain these facilities.

Two months later, in November 2013, the International Security Assistance Force issued a fragmentary order to reduce the size of the ANDSF infrastructure inventory by terminating, de-scoping, or offsetting ongoing construction projects less than 50 percent complete, giving the Afghan government a better chance of sustaining the remaining facilities.[42] As noted in our 2015 audit report on the status of our recommendations to DOD, this resulted in DOD discontinuing construction on all or part of 101 projects, achieving estimated cost savings of up to $800 million.[43]

Despite these actions, our concerns about the sustainability of facilities and infrastructure DOD has built for the Afghans persist.[44] In October 2013, we reported that the Archi Police District Headquarters, which had an estimated 40 ANP personnel living on site, had several facilities that were in disrepair, causing health concerns.[45] For example, we found extensive mold growing on the interior walls and ceilings of the barracks and bathrooms. In addition, the bathrooms were virtually unusable because of missing sink faucets, showers in disrepair, and no running water. Also, although a large generator had been installed at the site, at the time of our inspection, ANP personnel told us it had not been functional for the past 2 years because it needed repair. They added that even if the generator was repaired, they did not receive enough fuel to operate it. Instead, electrical power was being supplied by a small back-up generator, which ANP personnel said they purchased locally, that only provided the facility with 3 hours of electricity per day.

In our upcoming inspection report on the Afghan Air Force University, we found that the Afghan government has not properly maintained the buildings that USACE has transferred to

---

[42] International Security Assistance Force Fragmentary Order 215-2013, November 2013.

[43] SIGAR 15-29-AR, *Department of Defense: More than 75 Percent of All SIGAR Audit and Inspection Report Recommendations Have Been Implemented*, January 15, 2015.

[44] We have an ongoing audit examining the Afghan government's ability to sustain ANDSF facilities and infrastructure DOD has transferred to it. These include facilities and infrastructure built specifically for the ANSDF and facilities initially used by the U.S. and coalition forces.

[45] Inspection 14-5-IP, *Archi District Police Headquarters: Extensive Mold, Lack of Running Water, and Inoperable Electrical Systems Show Facilities Are Not Being Sustained*, October 20, 2013.

it.[46] Some of the bathroom buildings were only being partially used due to broken sinks, faucets, and water heaters. In addition, two of the renovated barracks buildings were not being used due to multiple problems, such as plumbing leaks and broken ceiling fans. We found other building problems, which could be mostly attributable to inadequate maintenance by the Afghan government, including mold growth, filthy bathrooms, broken door locks, and broken or missing plumbing fixtures.

Conclusion

Since 2008, SIGAR has issued 37 inspection reports examining 45 DOD reconstruction projects in Afghanistan with a combined value of about $1.1 billion. While some of the projects were well built and met contract requirements and technical specifications, most did not meet those requirements and specifications, and some of those had serious construction deficiencies that, in some cases, had health and safety implications. In many cases, poorly prepared or unqualified contractor personnel, inferior materials, poor workmanship, and inadequate contractor and U.S. government oversight contributed to those substandard results. Despite these problems, many contractors were still paid the full contract amount.

We recognize DOD's efforts to address our recommendations in a timely manner, and in ways that help improve the efficiency and effectiveness of reconstruction projects. Although many of our recommendations were directed toward specific projects, DOD also established procedures that impact the full scope of its reconstruction projects. However, despite these efforts, many of the projects we inspected had significant deficiencies caused, in part, by common and recurring problems.

Based on our work, DOD can improve its administration and oversight of its reconstruction projects by, among other things, improving its project planning and design processes; ensuring contractors are qualified and capable of adhering to requirements; and conducting the oversight needed to ensure that facilities are built correctly and contractors are held accountable for their work. This would help to avoid the waste and delay that can come from having to fix or simply abandon deficient projects.

Further, we continue to be concerned about the Afghan government's ability to sustain the facilities DOD has built for it. DOD is currently providing operation and maintenance services at many ANDSF facilities across the country. Currently, it is unclear when the Afghan

---

[46] We are currently in the process of finalizing this report and plan to issue it before the end of March 2016.

government will be able to take over this responsibility. Until it is able to do so, U.S. taxpayer funds will continue to be expended to sustain the facilities DOD has built for the Afghans.

SIGAR will also continue to work with DOD and Congress as it continues to oversee the critical work the United States and its coalition partners are undertaking in Afghanistan.

Thank you for the opportunity to testify today. I look forward to answering your questions.

Appendix I - SIGAR Inspections of DOD Reconstruction Projects in Afghanistan

Table 1 lists the inspection reports SIGAR has issued on Department of Defense reconstruction projects in Afghanistan since July 2009.

Table 1 - SIGAR Inspection Reports Issued to Date

Report Number, Title, Date Issued, Original Contract Amount, Administering Agency, and Map Number	Findings	Recommendations, Responsible Entity, and Recommendation Status as of February 29, 2015
SIGAR Inspection 09-01, *Improvements to the Khowst City Electrical Power System: Safety and Sustainability Issues Were Not Adequately Addressed,* July 28, 2009 $1.57 Million Khowst Provincial Reconstruction Team Map #1	(1) Facility not built as required, but it is being used. (2) Contract 1 omitted several important project requirements; however, contract 2 effectively addressed project requirements. (3) Contractor 1 did not meet several requirements. (4) U.S. provincial reconstruction team's quality assurance was inadequate. (5) Afghan government may have difficulty operating and maintaining the city electrical power system.	(1) Correct the safety hazards and other technical deficiencies noted in this report. (Khowst Provincial Reconstruction Team; Closed-Not Implemented) (2) Assign qualified personnel to provide oversight of the follow-on Commander's Emergency Response Program (CERP) projects to correct safety hazards and technical deficiencies at the Khowst Power System. (Khowst Provincial Reconstruction Team; Closed-Not Implemented) (3) Provide training and mentoring of the power plant management and personnel to build capacity for addressing long-term maintenance and sustainability. (Khowst Provincial Reconstruction Team; Closed-Not Implemented) (4) Review other CERP projects to determine whether adequate project oversight, training and mentoring is being provided to build capacity for long-term project sustainability. (Khowst Provincial Reconstruction Team; Closed-Not Implemented)
SIGAR Inspection 09-02, *Mahmood Raqi to Nijrab Road Construction Project in Kapisa Province: Contract Requirements Met, But Sustainability Concerns Exist,* October 2, 2009 $6.60 Million Kapisa Provincial Reconstruction Team Map #2	(1) Facility was built as required, and it is being used. (2) Kapisa Province Ministry of Public Works lacks the capacity—equipment, material, or personnel—to maintain the road, once completed. (3) SIGAR estimates the lifetime of the road to be 5 years, unless an effective repair and maintenance program is implemented.	(1) Continue coordination with the U.S. Agency for International Development to include this road in the expanding Management and Operation Program and develop capacity for repairing and maintaining roads at the provincial level. (U.S. Forces-Afghanistan (USFOR-A); Closed-Not Implemented) (2) Provide information through the Combined Information Data Network Exchange system to give the U.S. Agency for International Development visibility of this project's details. (Kapisa Provincial Reconstruction Team; Closed-Not Implemented)
SIGAR Inspection 10-01, *Farukh Shah School Construction Project,*	(1) Facility was not built as required, and was not being used.	(1) Issue a follow-up contract to address the construction deficiencies noted in this report.

Kapisa Province: Project Completion Approved Before All Contract Requirements Met, October 26, 2009 $0.15 Million Kapisa Provincial Reconstruction Team Map #3	(2) Project was closed out with significant work remaining to be completed, specifically school building, latrine, guard house, power plant, hand pump, and site clean-up. (3) We identified significant design deficiencies, including improper grading and the absence of a retaining wall that we believe should have been included in the project's scope of work. (4) Project was delayed by 2 years, and provincial reconstruction team says the provincial director of education pressured it to turning over the school "as-is" because students and teachers were using an outdoor area for instruction.	(Kapisa Provincial Reconstruction Team; Closed-Not Implemented) (2) Place greater emphasis on developing detailed scopes of work that anticipate and address critical design issues that are particular to each construction project rather than relying solely on standard design plans. (Kapisa Provincial Reconstruction Team; Closed-Not Implemented)
SIGAR Inspection 10-02, *Abdul Manan Secondary School Construction Project in Kapisa Province: Insufficient Planning, Safety Problems, and Poor Quality Control Affect Project Results,* October 26, 2009 $0.25 Million Kapisa Provincial Reconstruction Team Map #4	(1) Facility was not built as required and was not being used. (2) Statement of Work did not include major construction elements, resulting in a contract modification and cost increase, and subsequent award that was determined to be in violation of CERP guidelines requiring contract termination and project re-bid. (3) Lack of standardized quality assurance guidelines for CERP-funded projects.	(1) Take action to correct the multiple deficiencies noted in this report. This should start with ensuring both the Statement of Work and the Design Plan for this project reflect specific construction requirements, such as site location and contractor capabilities. (USFOR-A and Kapisa Provincial Reconstruction Team; Closed-Not Implemented) (2) Develop standardized quality assurance guidelines that can be used to manage this and other CERP-funded projects. (USFOR-A and Kapisa Provincial Reconstruction Team; Closed-Not Implemented)
SIGAR Inspection 10-03, *Habib Rahman Secondary School Construction Project in Kapisa Province: Design and Safety Issues Require Attention,* October 26, 2009 $0.31 Million Kapisa Provincial Reconstruction Team Map #5	(1) Facility was not built as required, and was not being used. (2) We identified contract and design issues. Specifically, the contract did not require removal of the existing unfinished structure, lack of a reinforced retaining wall, and lack of necessary earth removal work. (3) Inadequate provincial reconstruction team management and quality assurance program that later improved.	(1) Initiate a follow-on CERP project to correct the design and safety deficiencies noted in this report. (USFOR-A and Kapisa Provincial Reconstruction Team; Closed-Not Implemented)
SIGAR Inspection 10-04, *Kohi Girls' School Construction Project in Kapisa Province: Construction Delays Resolved, But Safety*	(1) Facility was built as required, but was not being used.	(1) Develop a plan for the removal of war-related debris from areas adjacent to the Kohi Girls' School construction project. (Kapisa Provincial Reconstruction Team; Closed-Not Implemented)

Concerns Remain,
October 26, 2009

$0.22 Million

Kapisa Provincial
Reconstruction Team

Map #6

SIGAR Audit 10-07, *The Tojg Bridge Construction is Nearly Complete, but Several Contract Issues Need to Be Addressed*, March 1, 2010 $1.75 Million Farah Provincial Reconstruction Team Map #7	(1) Facility was not built as required, and was not being used. (2) Concrete testing and other quality control measures were inadequate to ensure structural integrity of bridge. (3) Land ownership rights to bridge approaches were not documented. (4) Sustainability a concern in that local Afghan public works department lacks funding, equipment, and personnel.	(1) Establish accountability for the gravel plant and associated equipment to ensure the plant's sustainability. (USFOR-A and International Security Assistance Force (ISAF); Closed-Implemented) (2) Ensure that necessary quality control and quality assurance procedures are performed and adequately documented, including (a) testing of critical construction materials is completed, (b) the structural concrete meets design requirements, and, (c) preparation of weekly engineer reports documenting quality control and corrective actions. (USFOR-A and ISAF; Closed-Implemented) (3) Ensure land rights associated with the bridge approaches are documented and transferred to the Afghan government. (USFOR-A and ISAF; Closed-Implemented) (4) Address deficiencies in the contract files per applicable guidance. (USFOR-A and ISAF; Closed-Implemented)
SIGAR Audit 10-09, *ANA Garrison at Kunduz Does Not Meet All Quality and Oversight Requirements; Serious Soil Issues Need to Be Addressed*, April 30, 2010 $72.80 Million U.S. Army Corps of Engineers (USACE) Map #8	(1) Facility was not built as required, and was not being used. (2) Severe settling of soil was damaging buildings. (3) Poor welds and rust could lead to roof failure. (4) North Atlantic Treaty Organization Training Mission–Afghanistan/Combined Security Transition Command–Afghanistan (CSTC-A) officials were unaware of any justifications or planning documents for the garrison that addressed the strategic deployment of troops, garrisons, locations, or operations; however, the planning reports reviewed did not address these matters. (5) North Atlantic Treaty Organization Training Mission–Afghanistan/CSTC-A officials stated that the Afghan government does not have financial or technical capacity to sustain the Kunduz	(1) Repair the welds and mitigate the rust on steel supports on the affected structures. (USACE; Closed-Implemented) (2) Resolve the soil stability issue and determine what mitigation or corrective actions are required for DynCorp to complete the garrison, including ensuring that the site is properly graded. (USACE; Closed-Not Implemented) (3) Ensure the Kunduz garrison's contract files are maintained according to USACE guidance. (USACE; Closed-Implemented)

	garrison or other Afghan National Security Forces (ANSF) facilities.	
SIGAR Audit 10-10, *ANA Garrison at Gamberi Appears Well Built Overall but Some Construction Issues Need to Be Addressed*, April 30, 2010 $129.80 Million USACE Map #9	(1) Facility was built as required, but was not being used. (2) Facility appears well built, but poor flood control measures and site grading could lead to problems. (3) Concrete deck of the short bridge near the garrison's entrance is eroding. (4) North Atlantic Treaty Organization Training Mission–Afghanistan/CSTC-A officials stated they were unaware of any justification or planning documents for garrison's use. (5) Afghan government does not have capacity to sustain the Gamberi garrison or ANSF facilities.	(1) Mitigate silt accumulation in the anti-vehicle and flood control trench. (USACE; Closed-Implemented) (2) Ensure that the site is properly graded. (USACE; Closed-Not Implemented) (3) Repair bridge near the main entrance to the garrison. (USACE; Closed-Implemented) (4) Secure the weapons training range with a perimeter fence. (USACE; Closed-Implemented)
SIGAR Audit 10-12, *ANP Compound at Kandahar Generally Met Contract Terms but Has Project Planning, Oversight, and Sustainability Issues*, July 22, 2010 $45.00 Million USACE Map #10	(1) Facility was built as required, but was not being used. (2) Four projects completed, but delays ranged from 6 months to 2 years. (3) No construction issues revealed. (4) Inadequate project planning and oversight affected all four projects. (5) Afghan government does not have the financial or technical capacity to sustain ANSF facilities once they are completed.	(1) Ensure that future projects adhere to USACE's established quality assurance and quality control procedures. (USACE; Closed-Implemented) (2) Review and update current guidance on austere construction standards to include more detailed guidance regarding heating and cooling options for various types of facilities, with the option to allow for regional differences. (Combined Security Transition Command-Afghanistan (CSTC-A), in consultation with USACE; Closed-Implemented) (3) Provide guidance regarding appropriate electrical, plumbing, and other fixtures for facilities. (CSTC-A; Closed-Implemented)
SIGAR Audit 10-14, *ANA Garrison at Farah Appeared Well Built Overall but Some Construction Issues Should Be Addressed*, July 30, 2010 $68.10 Million USACE Map #11	(1) Facility not built as required, but it was being used. (2) Phase I completed 16 months past original completion date, and Phase II is 12 months behind schedule. (3) Contract management and oversight met requirements. (4) Afghan government does not have the financial or technical capacity to sustain all ANSF facilities; therefore, two contracts were being awarded to provide operations and maintenance for ANSF facilities.	(1) Ensure that the site is properly graded around buildings to prevent the pooling of water. (USACE; Closed-Implemented) (2) Ensure that the asphalt roads and parking lots are properly compacted to minimize deterioration. (USACE; Closed-Implemented) (3) Consider mitigating silt accumulation in the unlined drainage ditches around the garrison to minimize maintenance. (USACE; Closed-Implemented)

SIGAR Audit 11-03, *ANP District Headquarters Facilities in Helmand and Kandahar Provinces Have Significant Deficiencies Due to Lack of Oversight and Poor Contractor Performance,* October 27, 2010

Nad Ali ANP District Headquarters: $0.84 Million

Garm Ser ANP District Headquarters: $0.84 Million

Nahri Saraj ANP District Headquarters: $0.84 Million

Spin Boldak District Headquarters: $0.84 Million

Takha Pul District Headquarters: $0.84 Million

Zeheli ANP District Headquarters: $0.84 Million

Total: $5.88 Million[a]

USACE

Map #12 through #17

Our final inspection covered six sites. These findings applied to all sites.

(1) Construction was poor, and two suspension letters were issued.

(2) Project was for six Afghan National Police (ANP) facilities: one site turned over to the ANP, another site cleared for turnover, nominal progress on another site, and three sites remain idle.

(3) Almost all performance payments have been paid out, and minimal funds were withheld from contractor payments to cover deficient work.

Individual site findings were as follows:

(1) Nad Ali ANP District Headquarters: Facility was not built as required, but it was being used.

(2) Nahri Saraj ANP District Headquarters: Facility was not built as required, but it was being used.

(3) Spin Boldak District Headquarters Facility was not built as required, and it was not being used.

(4) Takha Pul District Headquarters Facility was not built as required, and it was not being used.

(5) Zeheli ANP District Headquarters Facility was not built as required, and it was not being used.

(6) Garm Ser ANP District Headquarters Facility was not built as required, and it was not being used.

Our final inspection covered six sites. These recommendations applied to all sites.

(1) Perform complete engineering evaluations at each of the six ANP project sites to determine the required level of reconstruction and repair needed to comply with the contract requirements. (USACE; Closed-Implemented)

(2) Pursue all available options to obtain necessary repairs by Basirat or recoup costs if the repairs are not made. (USACE; Closed-Implemented)

(3) Require that the maximum amount of retainage allowable by the Federal Acquisition Regulation (10 percent) be withheld from each payment for projects where information on the construction progress and quality is obtained primarily through the contractor or Local National Quality Assurance reports and where the contracting officer determines that satisfactory progress has not been made. (USACE; Closed-Implemented)

(4) Institute a requirement for USACE personnel to conduct site visits and verify payments for construction progress if the completed work has only been verified by photographs taken by the contractor or where the information provided by the reports does not meet USACE quality assurance reporting standards. (USACE; Closed-Implemented)

(5) Ensure compliance with USACE quality assurance standards on this and related projects, by directing Afghanistan Engineering District-South to require quality assurance representatives to file daily reports, ensure three-phase testing is implemented, and perform and record quality control testing. (USACE; Closed-Implemented)

(6) Direct Afghanistan Engineering District-South to develop a process and procedure for coordinating with local coalition force units to (a) help confirm construction progress claims, and (b) determine the feasibility of using coalition force assets to supplement security and transportation needs. (USACE; Closed-Implemented)

SIGAR Audit 11-09, *ANA Facilities at Mazar-e-Sharif and Herat Generally Met Construction Requirements, but Contractor Oversight Should Be Strengthened,* April 25, 2011

Our inspection covered two sites—Mazar-e-Sharif and Herat—and each site had its own contractor—CH2M Hill and AMEC Earth and Environmental, Incorporated, respectively. These findings applied to both sites.

(1) The contractors experienced construction delays and cost increases—

Our inspection covered two sites. These recommendations applied to both sites.

(1) Establish and implement procedures, including specific deadlines, to ensure that contracting officers follow up on contractors' corrective action plans in a timely manner. (AFCEE; Closed-Implemented)

Camp Shaheen: $17.00 Million

Afghan National Army (ANA) facilities at Camp Zafar: $11.60 Million

Total: $28.60 Million

Air Force Center for Engineering and the Environment (AFCEE)

Map #18 and #19

75 percent schedule growth and an estimated cost overrun of $1.68 million—because AFCEE did not exercise adequate contractor oversight.

(2) The quality of construction at both sites generally met the contract requirements.

Individual site findings were as follows:

(1) Camp Shaheen: Facility was built as required and was being used.

(2) ANA facilities at Camp Zafar: Facility was built as required and was being used.

(2) Take immediate action to finalize the performance rating of AMEC Earth and Environmental, Incorporated, the prime contractor at Camp Zafar, and add this rating to the Construction Contractor Appraisal Support System. (AFCEE; Closed-Implemented)

SIGAR Inspection 12-1, *Construction Deficiencies at Afghan Border Police Bases Put $19 Million Investment at Risk*, July 30, 2012 Lal Por 1: $4.55 Million Lal Por 2: $4.48 Million Nazyan Base: $4.77 Million Total: $13.80 Million USACE Map #20, #21, and #22	Our inspection covered three sites. This finding applied to all sites. (1) USACE failed to follow its quality control and assurance processes, and, primarily due to security concerns, did not verify that construction at the bases had been completed prior to acceptance and transfer to CSTC-A. Individual site findings were as follows: Lal Por 1: (1) Facility was not built as required, but it was being used. (2) We observed various construction deficiencies. Lal Por 2: (1) Facility was not built as required, and it was not being used. (2) The base had no viable water supply. (3) We observed various construction deficiencies. Nazyan Base: (1) Facility was not built as required, but it was being used. (2) The base may soon be uninhabitable if the septic system continues to back up into the pipes causing overflow. (3) We observed structural failures as a result of an inadequate drainage system. (4) Most facilities were either unoccupied or not used for their intended purpose.	Our inspection covered three sites. These recommendations applied to all sites. (1) Review the current status of construction deficiencies identified as part of the transfer of the bases, including the critical water supply and septic and sewage system deficiencies, and determine a resolution that is in the best interest of the U.S. government and without unnecessary additional government cost. (USACE; Closed-Implemented) (2) Determine the method of repair for the deficiencies still outstanding, including (a) remediation by the contractor, as part of complying with the contract terms; (b) recovery under warranty, as stipulated in the contract remediation timeframes and warranty terms; and (c) determining whether retainage and liquidated damages should be released to the contractor as part of contract closeout. (USACE: Closed-Implemented) (3) Based on the determination in recommendation 1, prepare a plan of action for the repairs and ensure the repairs are completed, inspected, and approved as expediently as possible. (USACE; Closed-Implemented) (4) For ongoing and future construction contracts, adhere to Federal Acquisition Regulation requirements and USACE Engineering Regulation 1180-1-6 for effectively managing a Quality Management Program, by ensuring that (a) each USACE Resident/Area Office is aware of and has access to the applicable Quality Assurance Surveillance Plan; (b) the contractor has developed an effective Contractor Quality Control Program, which is adequately monitored and assessed through the Quality Assurance Program; (c) construction deficiencies are tracked and remedied in a timely manner, to ensure quality construction is delivered at project completion, as part of the transfer process; and (d) per the terms of the transfer process, the Road & Roof Construction Company provides the requisite operations and maintenance manuals as well as the appropriate technical documents and training required for safe and effective operation of the facilities. (USACE; Closed-Implemented)
SIGAR Audit 12-02, *Better Planning and Oversight Could Have Reduced Construction Delays and*	(1) Facility was not built as required, but it was being used.	(1) Direct that site surveys done in conjunction with the Kabul Military Training Center conceptual master plan be more detailed, including topography and location of existing utilities, so that a more

Costs at the Kabul Military Training Center, October 26, 2011 $140.00 Million AFCEE Map #23	(2) The project (Phase III) was not completed. The project experienced both cost growth and schedule delays. (3) Some completed facilities were not being used as intended. Due to the expanded number of recruits, a gymnasium was being used for housing. (4) The Afghan government does not have the financial or technical capacity to sustain the center once completed.	complete picture of additional construction projects can be provided to bidders, thus allowing contract proposals to more accurately reflect reality. We support CSTC-A's efforts to develop the organic capability to do this and in the interim recommend that CSTC-A, in concert with AFCEE, use existing planning contracts to provide the integration function. (CSTC-A; Closed-Implemented) (2) Ensure that conceptual master plans for future construction projects in support of the ANSF contain more detailed information, including topography and the location of existing utilities, to facilitate the preparation of more accurate contract proposals. (CSTC-A; Closed-Implemented) (3) Ensure that, in the future, Kabul Military Training Center contract and task order files contain complete and consistent information regarding reasons for modifications to the contract and task orders. (AFCEE; Closed-Implemented) (4) Seek reimbursement from the Phase I and II contractor, AMEC Earth and Environmental, Incorporated, for the cost of electrical repairs related to poor performance by its Afghan subcontractors. (AFCEE; Closed-Implemented)
SIGAR Audit 12-03, *Afghan National Security University Has Experienced Cost Growth and Schedule Delays, and Contract Administration Needs Improvement*, October 26, 2011 $170.00 Million AFCEE Map #24	(1) Facility was built as required, but it was not being used. (2) Construction (Phase I) was not completed, and the project has experienced cost growth and schedule delays. However, the quality of construction at the University generally met contract requirements.	(1) Assure that, in the future, the Afghan National Security University task order file is complete, including complete and consistent documentation as to the reasons for task order modifications and that all notices to proceed are included in the contract files, and consider expanding the practice to all CSTC-A funded task order files. (AFCEE; Closed-Implemented) (2) Assure that out-of-scope modifications are properly justified, approved, and documented. (AFCEE; Closed-Implemented)
SIGAR Inspection 13-1, *Kunduz ANA Garrison: Army Corps of Engineers Released Dyncorp of All Contractual Obligations Despite Poor Performance and Structural Failures*, October 25, 2012 $55.50 Million USACE Map #25	(1) Facility was not built as required, but it was being used. (2) Subsequent SIGAR review determined ongoing problem of failed structures, potential structural failure, and severe soil settling and grading issues. (3) Inadequate construction quality and noncompliance with contract specifications. (4) USACE released the contractor from any further contractual obligations without requiring the contractor to provide	(1) Justify the cost of further repairs and remediation of structural failures at Camp Pamir funded with Afghan Security Forces Fund appropriations to ensure that further construction is warranted, at reasonable cost to the U.S. government. (USACE; Closed-Implemented) (2) Submit the DynCorp settlement to an appropriate audit agency for review, in accordance with Federal Acquisition Regulation 49.107(a). Based on the review, the audit agency should submit written comments and recommendations. While the audit results would normally be communicated to the termination contracting

	remediation of structural failures that will require additional funding above the $72.8 million paid to the contractor.	officer, due to the questionable nature of the settlement, we further recommend that the audit results and recommendations be reviewed by the Commanding General. (USACE; Closed-Implemented) (3) Explain in writing why the settlement was determined to be fair and reasonable. (UASCE; Closed-Implemented)
SIGAR Inspection 13-2, *Wardak Province National Police Training Center: Contract Requirements Generally Met, but Deficiencies and Maintenance Issues Need to Be Addressed*, October 30, 2012 $96.10 Million USACE Map #26	(1) Facility was built as required, and was being used. (2) Buildings and facilities were generally used as intended and constructed in accordance with contract specifications.	(1) Replace diesel fuel tank grounding connections with those specified in the design documents to avoid a potentially dangerous condition. (USACE; Closed-Implemented) (2) Repair roof leaks around the vehicle exhaust ventilation pipes in the vehicle maintenance building. (USACE; Closed-Implemented) (3) Repair the missing storm water outlet grating in the perimeter wall, which could enable a person to gain unauthorized access to the compound. (USACE; Closed-Implemented) (4) Regularly clean silt and construction debris from the storm drain system. (USACE; Closed-Implemented)
SIGAR Inspection 13-3, *Gamberi Afghan National Army Garrison: Site Grading and Infrastructure Maintenance Problems Put Facilities at Risk*, October 30, 2012 $126.50 Million USACE Map #27	(1) Facility was not built as required, but it was being used. (2) Sustaining the Gamberi ANA Garrison continues to be at risk due to the lack of remediation for ongoing flood control issues and inadequate grading.	(1) Repair damaged storm water facilities by repairing eroding ditches and removing sediment and debris on roads, in ditches, and in perimeter wall outlets throughout the garrison. (USACE; Closed-Implemented) (2) Implement mitigating flood control measures, such as adding gravel to low lying roads where flooding regularly occurs to drain these areas more quickly. (USACE; Closed-Implemented) (3) Establish and follow a program to maintain the storm water drainage system and ensure that timely repairs are made to correct the deficiencies that we identified. (USACE; Closed-Implemented) (4) Conduct a structural analysis and design review of the culvert design package and take appropriate actions to correct any deficiencies identified. (USACE; Closed-Implemented)
SIGAR Inspection 13-4, *Kunduz Afghan National Police Provincial Headquarters: After Construction Delays and Cost Increases, Concerns Remain About the Facility's Usability and*	(1) Facility was built as required, but it was not being used. (2) Construction was only 50 percent complete, but what was completed appeared adequate. No personnel were occupying the facility.	(1) Provide electrical back-up at the lift station, such as an auxiliary electrical generator, to provide back-up power to continue pumping untreated sewage into the sewage treatment plant and help mitigate the potential for sewage overflow when the main generator is out of service for repair or

Sustainability, January 24, 2013 $12.40 Million USACE Map #28	(3 The facility's only source of electrical power is a single diesel generator with no back-up or alternate connection to the local electrical grid or other back-up electrical power supply. (4) The contractor was having problems with collapsible soil and sink holes on the project site.	maintenance or from unintended power outages. (USACE; Closed-Implemented) (2) Review the decision made at the start of the project to not connect the site to the local electrical grid and, as part of the review, conduct a cost-benefit and technical analysis. The review should factor in the high costs to purchase and deliver fuel to the site for the electrical generator, the capability of the local grid to provide adequate power for the site facilities and equipment, and the need for a back-up electrical system. Based on the results, if connection to the local power grid is not feasible, install a back-up site generator or otherwise provide an appropriate back-up electrical power system to prevent loss of electricity across the site when the primary generator is not working. (USACE; Closed-Implemented) (3) Award an operations and maintenance contract at project completion to ensure that the facility is appropriately maintained once occupied. (USACE; Closed-Implemented)
SIGAR Inspection 13-5, *Iman Sahib Border Police Company Headquarters in Kunduz Province: $7.3 Million Facility Sits Largely Unused*, January 29, 2013 $5.70 Million USACE Map #29	(1) Facility was built as required, and it was being used. (2) The facility sat largely unused. Only approximately 12 personnel were on site during the SIGAR site inspection, and on-site personnel were not aware of plans to move additional staff into the compound. (3) The facility lacks an emergency supply, e.g., a back-up generator. (4) There is no operation and maintenance contract for on-site facilities and equipment, nor are there plans to provide training to local Afghan personnel. (5) The wood-burning stoves were dismantled, and justifications provided conflicted with one another.	(1) Review plans for constructing Afghan Border Police facilities to determine whether site construction contracts can be downsized or facilities redesigned to reduce unnecessary costs or if facilities, including this location, are even needed; and provide an explanation of the review results. (USACE; Closed-Implemented) (2) Rather than relying solely on a single generator, determine the feasibility of installing a backup generator or connecting the site electrical system to the local power grid to prevent loss of electricity across the site when the primary generator is out of service for repair or maintenance or from unintended power outages, including lack of fuel. (USACE; Closed-Implemented) (3) Award an operations and maintenance contract or otherwise provide training to Afghan personnel to ensure that the facility is appropriately maintained after the withdrawal of coalition forces. (USACE; Closed-Implemented) (4) Determine why the Afghan Border Police dismantled the wood-burning stoves at Imam Sahib Border Police Company Headquarters and assess the need to provide wood-burning stoves at other facilities currently under construction or planned for construction in the future. (USACE; Closed-Implemented)

SIGAR Inspection 13-6, *Afghan National Police Main Road Security Company, Kunduz Province, Is Behind Schedule and May Not Be Sustainable*, April 17, 2013 $1.70 Million USACE Map #30	(1) Facility was not built as required, and it was not being used. (2) One generator provides all of the compound's electricity, and the contract scope of work has no provision for a back-up generator or connection to the municipal power grid. (3) The Afghan power grid was inadequate for the facility's current demand and significant investment was required to connect to the national grid. (4) The project was behind schedule. At the time of our site visit, 54 percent of the performance period had passed but only 15 percent of the work had been completed.	(1) Review the ANP Main Road Security Company site design and install a back-up power system, at least for mission critical systems, to prevent loss of site electricity when the primary generator is out of service for repair or maintenance or from unintended power outages, including the lack of fuel. (USACE; Closed-Not Implemented) (2) Determine an appropriate means for ensuring operation and maintenance of the compound at project completion, and that the site is appropriately maintained as part of the turnover to the Afghan government. (USACE; Closed-Implemented)
SIGAR Inspection 13-7, *Qala-i-Muslim Medical Clinic: Serving The Community Well, But Construction Quality Could Not Be Fully Assessed*, April 17, 2013 $0.16 Million Joint Task Force-Kabul Map #31	(1) Facility was built as required, and it was being used. (2) The facility was being used for its intended purposes, and enhanced the medical capabilities of the Village. (3) Ministry of Public Health was fulfilling its commitment to sustain the medical clinic. (4) No major construction issues were observed.	(1) Ensure that project documentation related to CERP projects complies with CERP guidance. (USFOR-A; Closed-Implemented) (2) Periodically review the Combined Information Data Network Exchange database to ensure that all required project documents are uploaded into the database. (USFOR-A; Closed-Implemented)
SIGAR Inspection 13-8, *Forward Operating Base Salerno: Inadequate Planning Resulted in $5 Million Spent for Unused Incinerators and the Continued Use of Potentially Hazardous Open-Air Burn Pit Operations*, April 25, 2013 $5.40 Million USACE Map #32	(1) Facility was built as required, but it was not being used. (2) Inadequate planning resulted in incinerators and supporting facilities that will never be used, or, if used, do not have adequate capacity to provide for the complete disposal of the facility's solid waste. (3) The incinerators were not being maintained due to excessive operation and maintenance costs, and had fallen into disrepair.	(1) Take appropriate measures to prevent a reoccurrence of stagnant water at the Forward Operating Base Salerno incinerator facility. (USFOR-A; Closed-Implemented) (2) Expedite the contract for solid waste removal to facilitate the earlier cessation of open-air burn pit operations. (USFOR-A; Closed-Implemented) (3) Develop a list of disposition options for the Forward Operating Base Salerno incinerators, determine the most cost effective option for the U.S. government, and provide SIGAR the results within 60 days. (USFOR-A; Closed-Implemented)
SIGAR Inspection 13-10, *Bathkhak School: Unauthorized Contract Design Changes and Poor Construction Could*	(1) Facility was not built as required, and it was not being used. (2) Afghan ministry officials modified the construction contract without consulting with or obtaining the approval of the U.S. contracting officer.	(1) Prior to turning over the facilities to the Afghans, perform an immediate physical inspection of the two new school buildings, including appropriate engineering tests and analyses, and determine whether to certify the structural integrity of the buildings. (USFOR-A; Closed-Implemented)

Compromise Structural Integrity, July 24, 2013 $0.26 Million Regional Contracting Command-Central Map #33	(3) Poor planning and construction resulted in a structurally deficient school building being constructed in an earthquake-prone area.	(2) Require the contractor to correct any deficiencies or substandard work identified during the physical inspection and tests. (USFOR-A; Closed-Implemented) (3) Review the product substitutions made, and, based on a price analysis, determine whether the changes warrant a reduction in the overall cost of the contract. (USFOR-A; Closed-Implemented) (4) Identify the contracting officer(s) responsible for initial oversight of the Bathkhak school construction activities and determine why (a) no oversight visits were made during the first 6 months of construction; (b) no contract modifications were made approving the contractor's substitution of building materials; and (c) no pricing determinations were made of the building materials substituted for those required in the contract. After making these determinations, decide what disciplinary action, if any, should be taken against the contracting officer(s) responsible for not properly overseeing construction activities. (USFOR-A; Closed-Implemented)
SIGAR 14-5-IP, *Archi District Police Headquarters: Extensive Mold, Lack of Running Water, and Inoperable Electrical Systems Show Facilities Are Not Being Sustained*, October 20, 2013 $0.29 Million USACE Map #34	(1) Facility was built as required, and it was being used. (2) The facilities were not being maintained and were in a state of disrepair, with an estimated 40 ANP personnel living and working in facilities with extensive mold growing on the interior walls and ceilings of the barracks and bathrooms. (3) The bathrooms were virtually unusable because of missing sink faucets and showers in disrepair. (4) The facility's water well no longer worked, requiring water to be trucked to the site daily. (5) The facility only had 3 hours of electricity per day, which was provided by a small back-up generator.	(1) Determine why U.S. funds provided to the Ministry of Interior for the operation and maintenance of ANP facilities since December 2012 have not been used to maintain the Archi District Police Headquarters and what corrective actions will be taken to ensure direct funds to the Ministry of Interior for operation and maintenance are used as intended, and report back to SIGAR within 90 days. (North Atlantic Treaty Organization Training Mission/CSTC-A; Closed-Implemented)
SIGAR 14-10-IP, *Walayatti Medical Clinic: Facility Was Not Constructed According to Design Specifications and Has Never Been Used*, October 30, 2013	(1) Facility was not built as required, and it was not being used. (2) The clinic was completed; however, it was empty and had never been used. (3) The Ministry of Public Health was not maintaining the clinic, even though Joint Task Force-Kabul and the Ministry of	(1) Take steps to assist the Afghan government in installing the equipment required under the CERP contract or suitable alternative equipment. (USFOR-A; Closed-Implemented) (2) Determine whether Walayatti medical clinic has been officially transferred to the Ministry of Public

$0.19 Million Joint Task Force-Kabul Map #35	Public Health signed an agreement for the ministry to staff and equip the clinic upon its official transfer to the Afghan government. Ministry officials said they were not aware of their responsibility to do so. U.S. government had failed to coordinate with the Ministry's Policy and Planning directorate and had not officially transferred the facility to the Afghan government.	Health and, if not, take immediate action to do so. (USFOR-A; Closed-Implemented) (3) Work with Ministry of Public Health to take appropriate action to equip, staff, and sustain the medical clinic for the Walayatti village inhabitants. (USFOR-A; Closed-Implemented)
SIGAR 14-13-IP, *Forward Operating Base Sharana: Poor Planning and Construction Resulted in $5.4 Million Spent for Inoperable Incinerators and Continued Use of Open-Air Burn Pits*, December 16, 2013 $5.60 Million USACE Map #36	(1) Facility was not built as required, and it was not being used. (2) Incinerators were not used 3 years after completion. (3) Contractor paid in full despite major construction deficiencies and delays, and without testing to see if incinerators were operational. (4) Even if operational, the two incinerators were built too close together and would have required extensive manual labor to load incinerators and remove ash. (5) As a result, base continued to use open-air burn pit in violation of regulations.	(1) Conduct an inquiry into the circumstances of the acceptance of the incinerator facility at Forward Operating Base Sharana and the payment of $5.4 million to the contractor. (USACE; Closed-Not Implemented) (2) Based on the results of this inquiry, determine if any action should be taken against the contracting officer(s). (USACE; Closed-Not Implemented)
SIGAR 14-31-IP, *Salang Hospital: Lack of Water and Power Severely Limits Hospital Services, and Major Construction Deficiencies Raise Safety Concerns*, January 29, 2014 $0.60 Million Regional Contracting Center-Bagram Map #37	(1) Facility was not built as required, but it was being used. (2) The hospital had no electricity or water. (3) Building was three times larger than designed. (4) Unenforced expansion joint in building makes hospital highly susceptible to earthquake damage. (5) Hospital treats about 70 patients daily, but does not provide many intended services like surgery and dental care.	(1) Identify the contracting officer(s) responsible for oversight of the Salang hospital construction activities and determine: (a) why the hospital was not built according to contract specifications and acceptable construction standards; and (b) what disciplinary action, if any, should be taken against the contracting officer(s) who failed to provide required oversight. (USFOR-A; Closed-Implemented) (2) Identify the CERP program manager(s) and project purchasing officer responsible for Salang hospital and determine why required documents were not placed in the Combined Information Data Network Exchange database. (USFOR-A; Closed-Implemented) (3) Perform a physical inspection of the building, including appropriate engineering tests and analyses, and, given its location in a high seismic activity zone, determine what corrections are required to ensure the structural integrity of the building. (USFOR-A; Closed-Implemented)

SIGAR 14-41-IP, *Camp Monitor: Most Construction Appears to Have Met Contract Requirements, but It Is Unclear if Facility is Being Used as Intended*, March 12, 2014 $3.93 Million Regional Contracting Center-Kabul Map #38	(1) Facility was not built as required, and it was not being used. (2) Barracks, administration building, and other structures appeared well-built. (3) Dining facility was not completed and contractor had abandoned project. (4) Camp Monitor was empty and unused at time of 2013 inspection. (5) Nine months later, U.S. Forces-Afghanistan (USFOR-A) informed SIGAR that remote camp was now in use by Afghan army, and the dining facility was being completed.	None
SIGAR 14-81-IP, *Shindand Airbase: Use of Open-Air Burn Pit Violated Department of Defense Regulations*, July 14, 2014 $5.91 Million USACE Map #39	(1) Facility was built as required, and it was being used. (2) Two incinerators built for U.S. use were being used after warranty repairs made. (3) Two incinerators installed for use by Afghan military were not being used. (4) Disposal of prohibited waste continued at a burn pit after incinerators were operational.	(1) Determine why the U.S. military continued to send its solid waste to the open-air burn pits at Shindand Airbase for 5 months after incinerators became fully operational. (U.S. Central Command; Closed-Implemented) (2) Determine why prohibited "covered" waste was burned in open-air burn pits at Shindand Airbase as early as January 2011 and why the Department of Defense (DOD) did not notify Congress, as required under Section 317 of the 2010 National Defense Authorization Act. (U.S. Central Command; Closed-Implemented)
SIGAR 14-82-IP, *Gereshk Cold and Dry Storage Facility: Quality of Construction Appears To Be Good, but The Facility Has Not Been Used to Date*, July 16, 2014 $2.89 Million USACE Map #40	(1) Facility was built as required, but it was not being used. (2) Project completion delayed by about 8 months due to threatened and actual Taliban violence.	(1) DOD's Task Force for Business and Stability Operations should ensure that before approving future investment projects of any kind, there are willing investor(s) capable of assuming ownership of and responsibility for maintaining constructed facilities, or, in the absence of investors, that the Afghan Ministry of Commerce and Industry is willing and able to assume those responsibilities itself. (Under Secretary of Defense for Policy; Closed-Implemented)
SIGAR 15-25-IP, *ANA Camp Commando Phase II: Power Plant and Fuel Point Not Fully Operational Nearly Two Years After Project Completion*, January 6, 2015 $15.10 Million USACE	(1) Facility was not built as required, but it was being used. (2) Power from new $7 million electrical plant limited to one quarter of intended maximum output because an unauthorized connection by Afghan army damaged plant. (3) Fuel station appeared well-built but fuel pumps were never used. (A second	(1) Determine the amount paid to the Phase II contractor for required work that was not completed on the camp's power plant and fuel point, and, where appropriate, recoup those funds. (USACE; Closed-Implemented) (2) Provide documentation showing that the power plant's electrical system has been fully tested and commissioned. (USACE; Closed-Implemented) (3) Determine the reason(s) why the ANA has not used the Phase II fuel point to dispense fuel for

Map #41	fuel station costing $1 million was built nearby and also was not being used.)	vehicles, and, based on the results, decide whether steps should be taken to make it operational. (USACE; Closed-Not Implemented)

(4) Determine the circumstances leading to the acceptance of the Phase II work as completed, with full payment made to the contractor, when known deficiencies existed. Based on the results, determine what disciplinary action, if any, should be taken against the contracting officer or contracting officer's representative. (USACE; Closed-Implemented) |
| SIGAR 15-27-IP, *Afghan Special Police Training Center's Dry Fire Range: Poor Contractor Performance and Poor Government Oversight Led to Project Failure*, January 13, 2015

$0.46 Million

Regional Contracting Center-Forward Operating Base Shank

Map #42 | (1) Facility was not built as required, but it was being used.

(2) The facility was used, but buildings began to disintegrate 4 months after construction because of substandard building materials and construction.

(3) Facility was demolished and was being rebuilt with Afghan government funds. | (1) Determine the extent to which Qesmatullah Nasrat Construction Company substituted building materials without authorization or did not complete work according to the contract requirements and, where appropriate, recoup those funds. (U.S. Central Command; Open)

(2) Identify the contracting officer and contracting officer's representatives responsible for oversight of the construction activities and determine:

  a. why the range was not built according to contract requirements and acceptable construction standards; and

  b. what disciplinary action should be taken against these contracting officials for failing to provide adequate oversight. (U.S. Central Command; Open) |
| SIGAR 15-51-IP, *Afghan National Army Slaughterhouse: Stalled Construction Project Was Terminated After $1.25 Million Spent*, April 20, 2015

$12.00 Million

USACE

Map #43 | (1) Facility was not built as required, and it was not being used.

(2) Project was terminated for convenience 9 months after construction began.

(3) A partially built security perimeter wall around a largely open field resulted.

(4) Termination came as a result of a separate DOD program reducing facility inventory. | None |
| SIGAR 15-74-IP, *$14.7 Million Warehouse Facility at Kandahar Airfield: Construction Delays Prevented Facility From Being Used as Intended*, July 15, 2015

$13.50 Million

USACE | (1) Facility was built as required, but it was not being used.

(2) Defense Logistics Agency warehouse facility was well constructed, with a few minor deficiencies.

(3) The project experienced delays due to poor performance of the first contractor.

(4) The construction contract price was higher than originally planned and | (1) Determine and identify, and report back to SIGAR within 90 days, who made the decision, and why, to allow contract modifications to be made and additional funds to be spent on the warehouses after the decision was made in August 2013 to end the Defense Logistics Agency's mission in Kandahar. (U.S. Central Command; Open) |

Map #44	continued to increase even after the U.S. Army, USFOR-A, and Defense Logistics Agency knew the facility was no longer needed. (5) Defense Logistics Agency never used the facility. The facility remained empty after it took custody, with a few minor exceptions.	
SIGAR 16-16-IP, Afghan Ministry of Defense Headquarters: $154.7 Million Building Appears Well Built, but Has Several Construction Issues that Should Be Assessed, February 11, 2016 $154.70 million Air Force Civil Air Force Civil Engineer Center Map #45	(1) Building was generally built as required and was being used. (2) Building had some design and structural deficiencies that could impact its structural integrity during an earthquake or prolonged periods of rain. (3) The project experienced delays due to the contractor's inability to gain access to the site and weather, security, and funding issues, which resulted in the project being completed almost 5 years longer than originally planned. (4) The construction contract price was over three times higher than originally planned.	(1) Assess the building's structural integrity where separation joints are not a continuous line from the bottom to the top of the building and the allowable building movement exceeds standards, and if needed, make deficient areas structurally sound. (CSTC-A; Open) (2) Assess the need for the installation of seismic lateral bracing on non-structural components suspended from the ceiling or floor above, such as heating/cooling equipment, duct work, dropped ceilings, electrical fixtures, and drain pipes. (CSTC-A; Open) (3) Install flexible connections across all separation joints of non-structural components, such as gypsum wall board, dropped ceilings, and drain pipes. (CSTC-A; Open) (4) Assess the integrity of lateral bracing, anchorage, isolation, and energy dissipation of all equipment for compliance with the contract's seismic requirements, and make deficient items compliant with the requirements. (CSTC-A; Open) (5) Assess the installed roof drainage system for compliance with the design documents and the International Building Code, and correct any deficiencies. (CSTC-A; Open)

Source: SIGAR analysis of inspection reports issued to date

Note: ^aThe total contract amount of $5.9 million included one facility, Bughran ANP District Headquarters ($0.84 million), that was later de-scoped from the contract and, as a result, was not included in our inspection.

Appendix II - Status of Department of Defense Construction Projects at the Time of SIGAR's Inspections

Table 2 lists our inspection reports on Department of Defense reconstruction projects in Afghanistan, along with information about whether the facilities were built as required and were being used at the time of our inspection.

Table 2 - SIGAR Inspection Reports, Along with Building and Usage Information

Report Number, Title, and Date Issued	Built as Required	Facilities Used
SIGAR Inspection 09-01, *Improvements to the Khowst City Electrical Power System: Safety and Sustainability Issues Were Not Adequately Addressed*, July 28, 2009	No	Yes
SIGAR Inspection 09-02, *Mahmood Raqi to Nijrab Road Construction Project in Kapisa Province: Contract Requirements Met, But Sustainability Concerns Exist*, October 2, 2009	Yes	Yes
SIGAR Inspection 10-01, *Farukh Shah School Construction Project, Kapisa Province: Project Completion Approved Before All Contract Requirements Met*, October 26, 2009	No	Yes
SIGAR Inspection 10-02, *Abdul Manan Secondary School Construction Project in Kapisa Province: Insufficient Planning, Safety Problems, and Poor Quality Control Affect Project Results*, October 26, 2009	No	No
SIGAR Inspection 10-03, *Habib Rahman Secondary School Construction Project in Kapisa Province: Design and Safety Issues Require Attention*, October 26, 2009	No	No*
SIGAR Inspection 10-04, *Kohi Girls' School Construction Project in Kapisa Province: Construction Delays Resolved, But Safety Concerns Remain*, October 26, 2009	Yes	No*
SIGAR Audit 10-07, *The Tojg Bridge Construction is Nearly Complete, but Several Contract Issues Need to Be Addressed*, March 1, 2010	No	No*
SIGAR Audit-10-09, *ANA Garrison at Kunduz Does Not Meet All Quality and Oversight Requirements; Serious Soil Issues Need to Be Addressed*, April 30, 2010	No	No
SIGAR Audit 10-10, *ANA Garrison at Gamberi Appears Well Built Overall but Some Construction Issues Need to Be Addressed*, April 30, 2010	Yes	No*
SIGAR Audit 10-12, *ANP Compound at Kandahar Generally Met Contract Terms but Has Project Planning, Oversight, and Sustainability Issues*, July 22, 2010	Yes	No
SIGAR Audit 10-14, *ANA Garrison at Farah Appeared Well Built Overall but Some Construction Issues Should Be Addressed*, July 30, 2010	No	Yes

SIGAR Audit 11-03, *ANP District Headquarters Facilities in Helmand and Kandahar Provinces Have Significant Deficiencies Due to Lack of Oversight and Poor Contractor Performance*, October 27, 2010		
Garm Ser Afghan National Police (ANP) District Headquarters	No	No
Nad Ali ANP Distrist Headquarters	No	Yes
Nahri Saraj ANP District Headquarters	No	Yes
Spin Boldak ANP District Headquarters	No	No
Takha Pul ANP District Headquarters	No	No
Zeheli ANP District Headquarters	No	No
SIGAR Audit 11-09, *ANA Facilities at Mazar-e-Sharif and Herat Generally Met Construction Requirements, but Contractor Oversight Should Be Strengthened*, April 25, 2011		
Afghan National Army (ANA) Facilities at Mazar-e-Sharif: Camp Shaheen	Yes	Yes
ANA Facilities at Herat: Camp Zafar	Yes	Yes
SIGAR Inspection-12-1, *Construction Deficiencies at Afghan Border Police Bases Put $19 Million Investment at Risk*, July 30, 2012		
Lal Por 1	No	Yes
Lal Por 2	No	No
Nayzan Base	No	Yes
SIGAR Audit 12-02, *Better Planning and Oversight Could Have Reduced Construction Delays and Costs at the Kabul Military Training Center*, October 26, 2011	No	Yes
SIGAR Audit 12-03, *Afghan National Security University Has Experienced Cost Growth and Schedule Delays, and Contract Administration Needs Improvement*, October 26, 2011	Yes	No
SIGAR Inspection 13-1, *Kunduz ANA Garrison: Army Corps of Engineers Released Dyncorp of All Contractual Obligations Despite Poor Performance and Structural Failures*, October 25, 2012	No	Yes
SIGAR Inspection 13-2, *Wardak Province National Police Training Center: Contract Requirements Generally Met, but Deficiencies and Maintenance Issues Need to Be Addressed*, October 30, 2012	Yes	Yes
SIGAR Inspection 13-3, *Gamberi Afghan National Army Garrison: Site Grading and Infrastructure Maintenance Problems Put Facilities at Risk*, October 30, 2012	No	Yes
SIGAR Inspection-13-4, *Kunduz Afghan National Police Provincial Headquarters: After Construction Delays and Cost Increases, Concerns Remain About the Facility's Usability and Sustainability*, January 24, 2013	Yes	No
SIGAR Inspection-13-5, *Iman Sahib Border Police Company Headquarters in Kunduz Province: $7.3 Million Facility Sits Largely Unused*, January 29, 2013	Yes	Yes

SIGAR Inspection 13-6, *Afghan National Police Main Road Security Company, Kunduz Province: Project Does Not Meet Construction Requirements, Is Behind Schedule, And May Not Be Sustainable*, April 17, 2013	No	No*
SIGAR Inspection 13-7, *Qala-i-Muslim Medical Clinic: Serving The Community Well, But Construction Quality Could Not Be Fully Assessed*, April 17, 2013	Yes	Yes
SIGAR Inspection 13-8, *Forward Operating Base Salerno: Inadequate Planning Resulted in $5 Million Spent for Unused Incinerators and the Continued Use of Potentially Hazardous Open-Air Burn Pit Operations*, April 25, 2013	Yes	No
SIGAR Inspection 13-10, *Bathkhak School: Unauthorized Contract Design Changes and Poor Construction Could Compromise Structural Integrity*, July 24, 2013	No	No*
SIGAR 14-5-IP, *Archi District Police Headquarters: Extensive Mold, Lack of Running Water, and Inoperable Electrical Systems Show Facilities Are Not Being Sustained*, October 20, 2013	Yes	Yes
SIGAR 14-10-IP, *Walayatti Medical Clinic: Facility Was Not Constructed According to Design Specifications and Has Never Been Used*, October 30, 2013	No	No
SIGAR 14-13-IP, *Forward Operating Base Sharana: Poor Planning and Construction Resulted in $5.4 Million Spent for Inoperable Incinerators and Continued Use of Open-Air Burn Pits*, December 16, 2013	No	No
SIGAR 14-31-IP, *Salang Hospital: Lack of Water and Power Severely Limits Hospital Services, and Major Construction Deficiencies Raise Safety Concerns*, January 29, 2014	No	Yes
SIGAR 14-41-IP, *Camp Monitor: Most Construction Appears to Have Met Contract Requirements, but It Is Unclear if Facility is Being Used as Intended*, March 12, 2014	No	No
SIGAR 14-81-IP, *Shindand Airbase: Use of Open-Air Burn Pit Violated Department of Defense Regulations*, July 14, 2014	Yes	Yes
SIGAR 14-82-IP, *Gereshk Cold and Dry Storage Facility: Quality of Construction Appears To Be Good, but The Facility Has Not Been Used to Date*, July 16, 2014	Yes	No
SIGAR 15-25-IP, *ANA Camp Commando Phase II: Power Plant and Fuel Point Not Fully Operational Nearly Two Years After Project Completion*, January 6, 2015	No	Yes
SIGAR 15-27-IP, *Afghan Special Police Training Center's Dry Fire Range: Poor Contractor Performance and Poor Government Oversight Led to Project Failure*, January 13, 2015	No	Yes
SIGAR 15-51-IP, *Afghan National Army Slaughterhouse: Stalled Construction Project Was Terminated After $1.25 Million Spent*, April 20, 2015	No	No